At David C Cook, we equip the local church around
the corner and around the globe to make disciples.
Come see how we are working together—go to
www.davidccook.com. Thank you!

DAVID C COOK

transforming lives together

SUDDENLY SiNGLE JOURNAL

SUDDENLY SiNGLE JOURNAL

PROCESSING YOUR FIRST
YEAR AFTER DIVORCE

KATHEY BATEY

DAVID **C** COOK

transforming lives together

SUDDENLY SINGLE JOURNAL
Published by David C Cook
4050 Lee Vance Drive
Colorado Springs, CO 80918 U.S.A.

David C Cook U.K., Kingsway Communications
Eastbourne, East Sussex BN23 6NT, England

The graphic circle C logo is a registered trademark of David C Cook.

ISBN 978-1-4347-1173-1
eISBN 978-0-8307-7276-6

The Team: Alice Crider, Amy Konyndyk, Diane Gardner,
Rachael Stevenson, Susan Murdock
Cover Design: Nick Lee
Cover Photo: Getty Images

Printed in the United States of America
First Edition 2018

1 2 3 4 5 6 7 8 9 10

012818

I will guide you along the best pathway for your life. I will advise you and watch over you.

Psalm 32:8 NLT

CONTENTS

INTRODUCTION

The first year after divorce can be precarious. It can be complex and, for some, the most difficult part of the divorce journey. The good news is, you only have to go through your "firsts" once. Sometimes, however, even the anticipation of certain dates brings up strong emotions or concerns. You may have to tolerate these sensations, distract yourself, plug your nose, walk through it in faith, or reassure yourself that "this will pass." It *will* pass, and you will look back and be grateful, knowing God brought you through it heartily and faithfully because you allowed Him to. You'll look back and see His faithful fingerprints all over your life.

WHY JOURNAL IT?

If the first year is often painful and difficult, why would you journal it when you want to forget it forever? Because journaling is a powerful tool that allows you to process what you are going through and better understand it. You can look back and see how far you've come. You will also recognize how God brought you through this year, even when you weren't able to see that in the moment. Journaling also gives you a sense of control when circumstances feel beyond your control. It provides a place to vent, process, and grieve so you don't keep emotional pain locked inside. And this journal in particular will prompt you to start shifting your perspective about your life.

This journal is set up to be user friendly and pressure free. It is intended to be a supportive tool for you not an expectation you have to meet. However, the more you fill out, the more you will see what is happening in your life that you might otherwise overlook. Embrace your feelings, embrace your life, and embrace this powerful time.

You will not go through this first year alone. God will be with you all the way, and He will lead you. This is an important time in your life and growth, and it is worth recording.

HOW TO USE THIS JOURNAL

This journal provides a place to have a voice, share joys and concerns, and express your vexation with your life. It is not the place to bring shame upon yourself, evaluate, judge, or hold yourself up to anyone else's expectations. *Suddenly Single: Rebuilding Your Life after Divorce* and *Suddenly Single Workbook: Building Your Future after Divorce* will help you evaluate and change your life, but this journal provides a free space to vent the unvoiceable. Pour out your thoughts, frustrations, anguish, joy, jokes, twisted thoughts, and tormented commentary. Let it all flow from the deepest part of you. Begin your healing journey on these pages.

Keep this journal in a secure place so you know it is safe to share and be vulnerable when you write in it. You will notice the journal is divided into twelve months and various sections. You may need to start in the middle of the book if that is when you initially begin your first-year journey. You may need to jump around at times, depending on what life events you're encountering along the way. There are several journal pages per month, plus key holidays. You may choose to journal once a week or write as you feel the need throughout the month. Begin wherever you need to, and write on whatever page is appropriate for the day you're living.

BEFORE YOU START

Seasons

Winter, spring, summer, or fall in themselves may bring on melancholy. If you know a certain season will hit you hardest, prepare and plan so the waves of emotion won't overtake you. Maybe you and your former spouse felt close and romantic during the winter months. Or was it springtime when you both ran in races or walked through certain life passages together? Maybe summer is now the time to change your routines and stroll through gardens or ride your bike through the woods. Volunteer at community races, plant a garden, teach children about growing vegetables, or redecorate your house to make it more your own. Plan the time in advance so it doesn't take you by surprise. Reinvent each season to stand for something new.

Summer Holidays—Memorial Day, Fourth of July, Labor Day

These times have unique traditions. What do you want to make out of them? For most of us, these holidays aren't as significant as Christmas or Thanksgiving. But still, traditions can stir up emotions. It's up to you to choose how much emphasis you wish to attach to them. Take a moment and decide—is it the traditional barbeque, or would you like to rewrite the routine?

Take advantage of the freedom you now have to design these holidays any way your heart desires. If you have children, create a new, exciting getaway to the beach or a campsite. Begin to look at these dates as opportunities to recreate and redesign your priorities and your life!

Your Birthday

This is your special day, so plan something you really want to do. It can be simple—buy your own cake, take yourself to a movie, or meet a friend for coffee. Go out and explore nature. Throw yourself a party. Buy yourself a present.

Your Former Spouse's Birthday

It will come, and the kids may attend a celebration. Look past the hurt to what is really important here; they need their other parent. Encourage your children to go for their sake. The healthier their relationship with both parents, the more emotionally healthy they will be. The dividends on this will play out for years afterward and the rest of your life.

The First Wedding or Family Funeral

Go if you are invited. You can go alone or take a friend. Go but don't linger. Prepare yourself ahead of time to give yourself an out. It's okay to cry in the parking lot. Decide how you will gracefully leave early if it is too much. Life goes on. Marriages and deaths reveal it.

The Kids' Birthdays

Look at this through your children's eyes. What would bless them through this tough year? Remember they need your time more than anything. Write words of love and affirmation in their cards.

Celebrate them by whatever means you feel does so with heart. If money is an issue, be creative. It is the thought that counts.

Wedding Anniversary

The grief can hit you hard on this date. Expect it, and then you won't be surprised. Plan a distracting activity, put it on the calendar, then do it. Pray through the day. Take a moment of gratitude for what good there once was in this relationship. Then lift your head, dust yourself off, and proceed into a new day.

Incidental Reminders

You may experience dates and small events that represent your favorite times with your former spouse. Your favorite restaurant, your favorite joke, or a favorite song. They will appear. Journal them during this first year. Give yourself grace. If memories or regrets bring tears, let them fall. They will cleanse you. This year is about cleansing and making new. Ask God to hold you and give you hope.

Special Occasions and Ordinary Days

Guard your heart. Memories may flood your mind, so select a few good ones from your life and let the other ones go. Ordinary days and special occasions will affect you differently. Grief can sneak up on you at any given time. Give the sorrow a minute, acknowledge it is there and is real. Special occasions will feel difficult, but they're part of the journey toward recovery. Ordinary days may feel empty or disorienting. It is okay to wrestle with your emotions. Take one day at a time, and next year will be easier.

Divorce Anniversary

Honor this date for the loss but also see it as a new beginning not only the end of something. Congratulate yourself on making it through the first year on your own. This is a huge milestone! You've made it through with God's help. Look up—the world is spinning; take a deep breath and a big step forward. The most difficult part is over, the divorce and the first year after it.

NEW YEAR'S DAY

"New Year, new you." Find the uniqueness of this year and embrace it with a sense of anticipation, hope, possibility, and promise. Dream a little. Permit yourself some childlike innocence and wonder, and take risks again. Find your laughter again; find your passion and your enthusiasm for living. The only one who can stop you this New Year is you. The rest of your life is waiting.

Today I'm feeling

Moments of struggle

Moments of joy or gratitude

My New Year goals

WINTER

The apostle Paul, imprisoned for preaching the gospel, asked his friend Timothy to come visit before winter, because winter can be desolate and dark. Paul needed encouragement; he needed someone to bring him a glimpse of spring and hope. So do we. In winter, we must have faith that spring will come. It won't last forever. It is just a season.

Come before winter.

—2 Timothy 4:21 ESV

My feelings about winter

My favorite thing about winter

How I'm reinventing winter

JANUARY

Joy and peace may seem far away during this time of upheaval. But they can be found. Use this month to discover a deeper trust in Christ through this unknown journey. He knows the way. Give this season to Him, and give yourself some peace.

May the God of hope fill you with all joy and peace as you trust in him,
so that you may overflow with hope by the power of the Holy Spirit.
—Romans 15:13

Challenges I'm facing

Possible solutions for the challenges

Successes to celebrate

JANUARY

Take the clean slate of January to plan and create the rest of the year. What do you want to do? Are your goals as dreamy as they are realistic? Can you take actions you can measure? Is this the year to really take control of the life you want? Ask, seek, knock, and then get busy exploring all God has for you. Time flies; make it fly toward your dreams.

Take delight in the LORD, and he will give you the desires of your heart.
—Psalm 37:4

Actions I'm taking toward my new life

JANUARY

Sometimes it seems like God is hiding. Perhaps He likes to play hide and seek. If you seek Him, you'll find him—in an early morning sunrise, a child's laughter, a hug from a friend, or a miracle of provision that only His hand could deliver. Look around your life. Where have you seen glimpses of God lately?

Glimpses of God

JANUARY

Is there such a thing as an ordinary day? Whether you're having a good day or a rough day, even ordinary days can be extraordinary if you're willing to acknowledge that God made them all.

This is the day that the LORD has made; let us rejoice and be glad in it.
—Psalm 118:24 ESV

Something that made me angry

Things that make me happy

FEBRUARY

You have as much opportunity to be successful in life as anyone. Search for new opportunities this month that will be your "time and chance" to create a new life.

I again saw under the sun that the race is not to the swift and the battle is not to the warriors, and neither is bread to the wise nor wealth to the discerning nor favor to men of ability; for time and chance overtake them all.
—Ecclesiastes 9:11 NASB

Challenges I'm facing

Possible solutions for the challenges

Successes to celebrate

FEBRUARY

Is it difficult to face the love month? Instead of ignoring it or becoming cynical, how about celebrating it? Immerse yourself in God's love for you, which is unequalled in any human form.

Moments of struggle

Moments of joy or gratitude

FEBRUARY

Doldrums often appear in February. But it is a prime time to work on goal setting, planning, and risk taking. Find opportunities to try a new challenge or event. Put yourself out there in a unique way this month and then congratulate yourself that you did!

Actions I'm taking toward my new life

FEBRUARY

VALENTINE'S DAY

Buy yourself some flowers (or a plant). Take yourself out. Eat chocolate. Celebrate the Creator of love and the abilty to show emotions and share feelings with others. "Jesus loves me this I know, for the Bible tells me so," says the song. It was true when you were a child, and it remains true now.

Today I'm feeling

Something wonderful that happened today

What I'm doing to take care of myself today

FEBRUARY

Do you have the time and energy to allow people to rent space in your head for free? You have your Father's business to do and your dreams and goals to pursue. Try making your mental space only available to love, peace, and hope. Forgiveness offered to someone else is a wonderful gift you can give yourself, and it will free up some space.

Something that made me angry

Things that make me happy

SPRING

Forget the former things; do not dwell on the past. See, I am doing a new thing! Now it springs up; do you not perceive it? I am making a way in the wilderness and streams in the wasteland.

—Isaiah 43:18–19

My feelings about spring

My favorite thing about spring

How I'm reinventing spring

MARCH

God longs to give us what we need. Approach Him with confidence. Make faith your new love language. Ask your requests in Jesus's name. Find mercy and grace to live simply; life is complicated enough during this transitional year.

> *Let us then approach God's throne of grace with confidence, so that we may receive mercy and find grace to help us in our time of need.*
> —Hebrews 4:16

Challenges I'm facing

Possible solutions for the challenges

Successes to celebrate

MARCH

And what does the LORD require of you? To act justly and to love mercy and to walk humbly with your God.

—Micah 6:8

You have your marching orders. Where will they take you? Start your plan.

Actions I'm taking toward my new life

MARCH

Pray once, then stretch your faith and pray again. Mustard-seed faith? It can move mountains. Mountain-size faith? It will rock your world.

I'm trusting God for

MARCH

Where's the lesson in this time of your life? This time is not in vain in God's economy. Where is your trust? In others? In yourself? In Him? Who is worthy of your trust? Honor this time as precious and important. You will never pass this way again.

Moments of struggle I've encountered

Moments of joy I've experienced

MARCH

Days come when your senses can't get it right, your emotions can't make it right, and your logic can't settle it. You just have to decide to let it go and carry on.

Something that makes me angry

Things that make me happy

APRIL

Simplify your life financially so you can have peace and confidence.

Keep your lives free from the love of money and be content with what you have, because God has said: "Never will I leave you, never will I forsake you." So we say with confidence, "The Lord is my helper; I will not be afraid. What can mere mortals do to me?"
—Hebrews 13:5–6

Challenges I'm facing financially

Possible solutions for the challenges

Successes to celebrate

APRIL

What's on the other side of this season of life? What blessings and growth await that you can't see and you find too difficult to pursue? God loves you too much to leave you where you are. Keep looking for the other side, the bigger picture. You will get there much faster with faith.

Moments of struggle

Moments of joy or gratitude

APRIL

Even little steps are progress. Don't underestimate what consistent, persistent small steps can make. They will get you where you want to go. It doesn't have to be drastic, just persistent.

Actions I'm taking toward my new future

APRIL

EASTER

The resurrection holds the essence of hope. Go to church, even if you are by yourself. Sit in wonder. Forget the people around you; listen to the songs and message as if God is reaching out to you alone. Listen for the victory. It wasn't just for a holiday. It was for you.

What I'm most grateful for

Glimpses of God in my life

APRIL

The challenge is to be angry but not be unkind. Gentleness is a powerful, often unused tool that requires patience. But it can be so effective in changing hearts. Use gentle words to lift up those who anger you. Use kind words to lift yourself up too.

Something that makes me angry

Things that make me happy

MAY

What do you need right now? Have you asked God for it? He is waiting for permission to enter your life.

Ask and it will be given to you; seek and you will find; knock and the door will be opened to you. For everyone who asks receives; the one who seeks finds; and to the one who knocks, the door will be opened.

—Matthew 7:7–8

Challenges I'm facing

Possible solutions to the challenges

Successes to celebrate

MAY

And here they come, those stubborn little flowers that ignore the death of winter. They are ignorant little things. Their faith in the sun forgets the snowy cold and all the dismal aspects of winter. Restoration, rebirth, resurrection. All of earth tells a story leading us back to God.

Moments of struggle

Moments of joy

MAY

What if the most important reason God still has you on earth is to pray for your loved ones? Never underestimate the great things He will do with your prayers. Pray seriously with a pleading heart. The prayers of the righteous are powerful and bring results.

People I'm praying for

MAY

MEMORIAL DAY

Remember those who died for you to keep you safe and to give you peace and freedom. Then turn your eyes toward heaven. When have you been the most grateful for the peace and freedom you enjoy? When have you most sensed your spiritual peace and freedom that comes through Christ?

> *Remember the former things, those of long ago; I am God, and there is no other; I am God, and there is none like me.*
>
> —Isaiah 46:9

Sweet lifetime memories

I'm trusting God for

MAY

Acknowledge how far God has brought you. Look up the word *rejoice* in the dictionary, understand its meaning, and then find ways to incorporate it into your life.

Then he turned my sorrow into joy! He took away my clothes of mourning and clothed me with joy.

—Psalm 30:11 TLB

Something that makes me angry

Things that make me happy

SUMMER

Breathe deeply. Look at the world in bloom again as if you are seeing it for the very first time. Is this the month for growth and flourishing? What makes your life colorful and beautiful?

> *All nature is within your hands; you make*
> *the summer and the winter too.*
> —Psalm 74:17 TLB

My feelings about summer

My favorite thing about summer

How I'm reinventing summer

JUNE

This month, find rest in prayer, and ask God to take you deeper in relationship with Him. He will never tell you no. He holds pleasures for you forevermore.

> *But when you pray, go into your room, close the door and*
> *pray to your Father, who is unseen. Then your Father,*
> *who sees what is done in secret, will reward you.*
> —Matthew 6:6

Challenges I'm facing

Possible solutions for the challenges

Successes to celebrate

JUNE

What should be June's theme? Is it the month for boldness? For breaking out into your new life? Regardless of where you are in this first year after divorce, step out in faith and see what will happen.

Moments of struggle

Moments of joy or gratitude

JUNE

What needs to go? Maybe it's you. Maybe your surroundings don't fit you anymore. Maybe you are trying to wear your old life while trying to create a new one. Let go of what doesn't fit anymore. Purge it.

Actions I'm taking toward my new life

What I'm letting go of

JUNE

Warmth comes in June. We seek warmth like we seek comfort. We hide our need; we don't want to be searching or vulnerable. But we all are. We are all vulnerable. Some of us just hide it better.

*Look to the L*ORD *and his strength; seek his face always.*
—1 Chronicles 16:11

Glimpses of God lately

I'm trusting God for

JUNE

Expectations can be killers—of relationships, of self-care, of dreams and goals. What expectations do you have for yourself? Are they too perfectionistic? Do they discourage you from trying because you expect too much too fast?

Something that makes me angry

Things that make me happy

JULY

We search in all the wrong places for what our soul needs. We long for peace and for freedom from the pain of the past. God holds it all. Seek His precepts (truth and principles); they will bless you and your children.

I will walk about in freedom, for I have sought out your precepts.

—Psalm 119:45

Challenges I'm facing

Possible solutions for the challenges

Successes to celebrate

JULY

Your divorce has cost too much already. You need wisdom so you don't lose any more time.

Teach us to number our days that we may gain a heart of wisdom.
—Psalm 90:12

Moments of struggle

Moments of joy or gratitude

JULY

INDEPENDENCE DAY

When do you feel the most free? Do you find your freedom in Christ? Are you free from debt? Worry? Self-sabotage? Shame and blame? Declare your freedom today.

Actions I'm taking toward my new life

JULY

Wow. God's ways work. The promises you trust prove themselves true. Write about how you have noticed this in your life.

I am most grateful for

Ways I'm letting go and trusting God

AUGUST

Because of the cross, we can focus on God's goodness and trust He will not remember all of our past mistakes and failures. Focus on how the Lord is good. Since He has forgiven you, don't you think it's time you forgive yourself?

Do not remember the sins of my youth and my rebellious ways;
according to your love remember me, for you, LORD, are good.

—Psalm 25:7

Challenges I'm facing

Possible solutions for the challenges

Successes to celebrate

AUGUST

When troubles come, when grief and confusion dominate, it's hard to be still and know God is God. When we least feel like being still and trusting, that is the hour God wants in.

Be still, and know that I am God; I will be exalted
among the nations, I will be exalted in the earth.

—Psalm 46:10

Moments of struggle

Moments of joy or gratitude

AUGUST

Determine who makes up your support network. Love everyone, but use discernment this year when deciding who enters into your personal space and life.

Above all else, guard your heart, for everything you do flows from it.
—Proverbs 4:23

Actions I'm taking toward my new life

AUGUST

God knows your heart's desires. He wants to give them to you and use them for His good purpose.

Take delight in the LORD, and he will give you the desires of your heart.

—Psalm 37:4

My heart's desire

Glimpses of God

AUGUST

What does it take to make an ordinary day extraordinary? It takes extra. Extra attention to detail. Extra sensitivity to what is important. God never meant for you to have an ordinary life, but an abundant and purposeful one. What and where are your extras?

Something that makes me angry

Things that make me happy

FALL

Unforgiveness can entangle you, lack of focus can distract you, and the pain of divorce can paralyze you. Like a heavy cloak, throw it all off. Life is too precious to waste any more time.

Let us throw off everything that hinders and the sin that so easily entangles. And let us run with perseverance the race marked out for us.
—Hebrews 12:1

My feelings about fall

My favorite thing about fall

How I'm reinventing fall

SEPTEMBER

The Lord hears you. You can rest. He is steady in these uncertain times, and He is in control. So, knowing He hears your voice, rest your soul.

I love the LORD, for he heard my voice; he heard my cry for mercy.
Because he turned his ear to me, I will call on him as long as I live....
Return to your rest, my soul, for the LORD has been good to you.

—Psalm 116:1–2, 7

Challenges I'm facing

Possible solutions for the challenges

Successes to celebrate

SEPTEMBER

LABOR DAY

What is your labor? Consider the work of your life and the legacy you want to leave behind. You might be closer to leaving that legacy than you think. Is this the month to sort out priorites and consider if you are living out what is most important to you?

Moments of struggle

Moments of joy or gratitude

SEPTEMBER

Your first year after divorce is also a spiritual journey. Has your worship become stale and routine, or have you really worshipped at all? Worship God in a new way. It will change you, revive you, and inspire you toward new actions in your life. If you have never worshipped God before, ask Him to show you how. Watch and listen for His response. He may answer it through prayer, Scriptures, or the spoken word of others.

Actions I'm taking toward my new life

SEPTEMBER

The simple things often end up being the greatest things—like peace, hope, and health. How do you see God providing for you in the areas of peace, hope, and health? How are you working toward these benefits?

Glimpses of God

I'm grateful for

SEPTEMBER

God sprinkles His kindness and love into your day in beautiful ways, and though some days you must strain to see them, they are there. If you focus on kindness and love, you will notice them, and they will dissolve some of your anger.

> *You fill my cup until it overflows. Your kindness and*
> *love will always be with me each day of my life.*
> —Psalm 23:5–6 CEV

Something that makes me angry

Things that make me happy

OCTOBER

You've come so far; there is much to gain from following faithfully and persistently. There is blessing on the other side of this year. Keep moving forward. God has so much in store for you. This year will settle; you will find your stride.

Let us not become weary in doing good, for at the proper
time we will reap a harvest if we do not give up.
—Galatians 6:9

Challenges I've encountered

Possible solutions for the challenges

Successes to celebrate

OCTOBER

As you redesign your life this year, examine your heart and character to see what is within you. What unfinished business is holding you back from living the life you want—finances, relationships, lack of forgiveness, fear, unbelief? What can you let go of?

Search me, God, and know my heart; test me
and know my anxious thoughts.
—Psalm 139:23

Moments of struggle

Moments of joy or gratitude

OCTOBER

Golden leaves, cooler nights, the gathering of crops—the world is going through change too. Life is always changing. You are not alone on your journey. Embrace your change; it is filled with abundant opportunity.

Actions I'm taking to move forward in my life

OCTOBER

Look around you and notice the harvests. What good things are you harvesting? What you sow you will harvest. Sow carefully into the hearts of others and you too will harvest and find God's calling.

I'm most grateful for

I'm looking forward to

OCTOBER

God's Spirit within us longs for things to be right and fair. You have experienced injustices in life. Are there some you need to surrender to God? Allow Him to be God in this area. Be wise, not vengeful. In doing so, you will give yourself peace.

Do not take revenge, my dear friends, but leave room for God's wrath, for it is written: "It is mine to avenge; I will repay," says the Lord.

—Romans 12:19

Something that makes me angry

Things that make me happy

NOVEMBER

God's will is unique to you. He rewards those who obey His call. This distinct call upon your life is one of fellowship between God and you. When you determine His calling on your life, follow it with all your heart. There you will find peace, joy, and purpose.

You need to persevere so that when you have done the
will of God, you will receive what he has promised.
—Hebrews 10:36

Challenges I'm facing

Possible solutions for the challenges

Successes to celebrate

NOVEMBER

What are the fears in your struggle? Identify your fears so you can take the power from them. Don't give fear control over what Christ has made free.

Moments of struggle

Moments of joy or gratitude

NOVEMBER

You can't steer a parked car. If you're unsure of what steps to take to begin the rest of your life, reach out to someone you trust. Seek counselors.

Get all the advice and instruction you can, so
you will be wise the rest of your life.
—Proverbs 19:20 NLT

Actions I'm taking toward my new life

NOVEMBER

THANKSGIVING

Gratitude expands our world. It makes us more content with what we have. If we understand the Source of our blessings, we can find the eternal purpose of them.

Give thanks in all circumstances; for this is
God's will for you in Christ Jesus.
—1 Thessalonians 5:18

I'm most grateful for

A new tradition I'd like to start

NOVEMBER

How do we control those loose thoughts that run fast and furiously through our minds? We take them captive to Christ. We submit them to Him when we can't handle or control them.

We destroy arguments and every lofty opinion raised against the knowledge of God, and take every thought captive to obey Christ.
—2 Corinthians 10:5 ESV

Something that makes me angry

Things that make me happy

DECEMBER

Christmas is God's gift that gives you life and purpose. Create new traditions as you determine which of the old ones you'll keep. Christmas will be whatever you make it. Make it something special, like you're celebrating it for the first time.

She will give birth to a son, and you are to give him the name Jesus, because he will save his people from their sins.
—Matthew 1:21

Challenges I'm facing

Possible solutions to the challenges

Successes to celebrate

DECEMBER

So often we forget God is for us. He wants to bless us and withholds no good thing from those He loves. Live this month like everything is working for you in God's favor.

Don't be afraid little flock, for your Father has
been pleased to give you the kingdom.
—Luke 12:32

Moments of struggle I've experienced lately

Moments of joy or gratitude

DECEMBER

In the rush of the holidays, find the quiet you need.

Be still, and know that I am God.

—Psalm 46:10

What I'm doing to take care of myself during this holiday season

New traditions I want to start

DECEMBER

CHRISTMAS DAY

Notice the lights because the Light has come into the world. Use the heightened sensitivity you feel to really hear the words of the carols, the words of the greetings, the words and actions of kindness and love. Find your own Christmas.

Moments of awe and wonder

I'm most grateful for

DECEMBER

*Finally, believers, whatever is true, whatever is honorable and worthy
of respect, whatever is right and confirmed by God's word, whatever
is pure and wholesome, whatever is lovely and brings peace, whatever
is admirable and of good repute; if there is any excellence, if there
is anything worthy of praise, think continually on these things
[center your mind on them, and implant them in your heart].*
—Philippians 4:8 AMP

Something that makes me angry

Things that make me happy

ANOTHER NEW YEAR

It's time to look forward! The past has passed; leave it there and allow God to take you into your future.

My New Year goals and dreams

By this time next year …

I will be

I will do

I will have

MY BIRTHDAY

God is jealous for you. He wants your attention and love. Consider the fact that God wants a relationship with you. Even in your challenges He longs to be with you. Doesn't that make you marvel and wonder?

> *For the LORD your God is a consuming fire, a jealous God.*
> —Deuteronomy 4:24

Challenges I've encountered lately

Successes I've enjoyed

MY BIRTHDAY

Celebrate you. Do something special that fills your heart. What do you really desire this birthday? Find some joy and celebrate your life.

Moments of struggle

Moments of joy or gratitude

MY BIRTHDAY

Make this your "I choose to make it happy" birthday.

Ways I'll take care of myself/treat myself today

Actions I'll take to make today special

MY BIRTHDAY

Watch for God. Thank Him for this birthday. Many people don't get to see this age or have this time to redesign their life and make it wonderful. Accept what is and make it beautiful. He is the best gift you will receive today. And the most personal one.

Glimpses of God in my life

I'm trusting God for

MY FORMER SPOUSE'S BIRTHDAY

In this first birthday apart, can you let go of your former spouse and bless his or her life? For your own peace, release your spouse into his or her new path. It is not what you planned, but life will go on. And releasing your former spouse will allow you to fill that space in your life with something good.

Moments of grief

Moments of gratitude

Glimpses of God in his or her life

MY WEDDING ANNIVERSARY

There should have been a celebration, but instead there is emptiness and pain. This date will always be in your mind when it comes around. The first anniversary after the divorce is the most difficult, but reflect on what was good in the past. Don't hold it in grief. Instead, pause, breathe, and even smile, for there once was a beautiful experience and something good still remains (maybe it's children, experiences or lessons).

Moments of grief

Moments of gratitude

Today I'll take care of myself by

MY WEDDING
ANNIVERSARY

*One thing I do: Forgetting what is behind and straining toward
what is ahead, I press on toward the goal to win the prize for
which God has called me heavenward in Christ Jesus.*

—Philippians 3:13–14

Challenges I'm facing today

Possible solutions to the challenges

Successes to celebrate

MY CHILD'S BIRTHDAY

This strange time will work itself out and not always be as awkward as it may seem today. Focusing on your child will make it easier to get through. Your child needs to see unity and consistency. Bless him or her by granting unity and peace.

Moments of grief

Moments of gratitude

MY CHILD'S BIRTHDAY

Challenges I'm facing

Possible solutions for the challenges

Successes to celebrate

MY CHILD'S BIRTHDAY

Moments of struggle

Moments of joy or gratitude

MY CHILD'S BIRTHDAY

Glimpses of God in my child's life

I'm praying and trusting God for

SPECIAL OCCASIONS: FIRST WEDDING

You may not feel like going, but go. Celebrate love and life and the future ahead for this couple. Pray for them. Rejoice with them. You have your own future ahead and it is full of beauty and potential too.

The first wedding I attended alone, I felt

Moments of grief

Moments of gratitude

SPECIAL OCCASIONS: CHILD'S GRADUATION

Moments of grief

Moments of gratitude

Struggles I encountered

Joys I experienced

SPECIAL OCCASIONS: FIRST FUNERAL

You may wonder if you should go. It may be awkward. If this person meant a great deal to you and you want to honor them, go. Pay your condolences and leave when appropriate. It will show you cared to pay respects and it will minimize the awkwardness and stress if you don't linger.

Attending a funeral for the first time without my spouse, I felt

Moments of grief

Moments of gratitude

Glimpses of God

NOT-SO-SPECIAL OCCASIONS: FIRST ENCOUNTERS

It's going to happen eventually—running into your former spouse. Hold your head up high and say, "Hello, nice to see you," and keep conversation to a minimal if it is difficult for you. You don't have to explain anything. The next run-in will be easier; you will find your stride.

When I saw our friends for the first time, I felt

Moments of grief

Moments of joy

What I can do to take care of myself

NOT-SO-SPECIAL OCCASIONS: SEEING SPOUSE WITH SOMEONE ELSE

This is difficult, but look at it as a challenge—one of strength that you are standing strong on your own and you have your own life . Focus on the good things, the strong things that are going well in your life. Focus there, not on them and not on the new partner.

When I saw my former spouse with someone else for the first time, I felt

Moments of grief

Moments of regret

What I can do to take care of myself

DREAMS AND GOALS

Dreams may be difficult to find during your first year after divorce. You'll spend more time recovering than dreaming, but start thinking toward this important part of your healing. Make time to dream and create new goals for yourself. Write them down along with any challenges you are facing.

A few goals

Challenges I'm facing

Possible solutions to the challenges

Successes to celebrate

DREAMS AND GOALS

Have you written down your dreams? Now begin to pencil in some ideas, some specific actions, to turn them into reality. Don't be afraid to make your thoughts bold. Everything great begins with an idea, and then the success depends on the actions taken toward them.

But those who hope in the LORD will renew their strength.
They will soar on wings like eagles; they will run and
not grow weary, they will walk and not be faint.
Isaiah 40:31

Actions I can take toward my dreams and goals

DREAMS AND GOALS

God put dreams in your heart and has given you gifts, and He has not changed His mind about them regardless of your marital status.

For the gifts and the calling of God are irrevocable [for He does not withdraw what He has given, nor does He change His mind about those to whom He gives His grace or to whom He sends His call].
—Romans 11:29 AMP

Glimpses of God

I'm trusting God for

MY DIVORCE ANNIVERSARY

Here you are. This "sticky" date on the calendar you've probably dreaded because you didn't know how you would feel or react when the day came. Consider it an accomplishment. You've made it this far. It wasn't easy, but it will get easier still. You're stronger than you thought you were and stronger because of where you are now. No one goes through this life event without changing. Make the change for the better. Be confident in Him who will not let go of you. Rest in Christ. He set you free. Explore what that means for you this coming year.

Therefore, there is now no condemnation for those who are in Christ Jesus, because through Christ Jesus the law of the Spirit who gives life has set you free from the law of sin and death.

—Romans 8:1–2

Moments of grief

Moments of gratitude

MY DIVORCE ANNIVERSARY

If the sting of injustice still aches in you or the pain of loss still has its grip, take a moment to allow peace to flow over you. Claim peace in Christ and ask Him to hold you even if you don't feel peace right now. Your story isn't finished. Find your support; don't go through this alone.

Challenges I'm facing

Possible solutions to the challenges

Successes to celebrate

MY DIVORCE ANNIVERSARY

*To every thing there is a season, and a time
to every purpose under the heaven.*

—Ecclesiastes 3:1 KJV

Moments of struggle

Moments of joy or gratitude

Glimpses of God

MY DIVORCE ANNIVERSARY

Consider what marvelous things God has in store for you when you act upon the foundation you built over the past year. You flushed out all the dross from your pain and your transition. You chose gratitude and the high road. You have a future ahead! God bless you; you have made it through one of your life's most difficult years. Don't stop now! Keep on with God. Watch for His presence and leading in your life. He has a plan, better than you could ever imagine for yourself.

Always giving thanks to God the Father for everything,
in the name of our Lord Jesus Christ.
—Ephesians 5:20

By this time next year, I will

Be

Do

Have

Use the following pages to journal any other thoughts, feelings, or prayers you have during this first year.

More **SUDDENLY SINGLE** resources

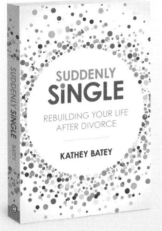

SUDDENLY SINGLE
A Compassionate Guide through the Challenges of Divorce

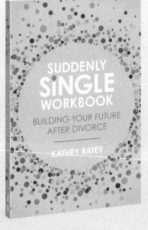

SUDDENLY SINGLE WORKBOOK
An Eight-Week Journey into Your New Life Story

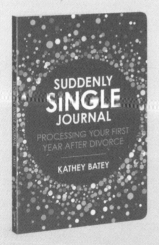

SUDDENLY SINGLE JOURNAL
A Place to Process, Plan, and Dream Again

Available wherever books are sold